WARNING!

THESE JOKES WILL ANNOY EVERYONE YOU KNOW AT CHRISTMAS

WARNING!

THESE JOKES WILL ANNOY EVERYONE YOU KNOW AT CHRISTMAS

PENGUIN BOOKS

CONTENTS

ELF EXTRAVAGANZA

How do you help someone who has lost their Christmas spirit?

Nurse them back to elf.

What is every elf's favourite type of music?

Wrap.

What do Santa's elves learn in school?

The elf-abet.

How do elves respond when Santa takes the roll?

'Present!'

How do the elves clean Santa's sleigh the day after Christmas?

They use Santa-tiser.

What do Santa's elves drive?

Mini vans.

What do you call an elf wearing earmuffs?

Anything you want – he can't hear you.

What kind of money do elves use at the North Pole?

Jingle bills.

What's an elf's favourite sport?

North Pole-vaulting.

What do you call an elf that runs away from Santa's workshop?

A rebel without a Claus.

Why do Santa's helpers have therapists?

They have low elf-esteem.

What do you call a greedy elf?

Elfish.

Why are elves such great motivational speakers?

They have plenty of elf-confidence.

What type of cars do elves drive?

Toy-otas.

What does Santa Claus do when his elves misbehave?

He gives them the sack.

What do elves use to make last-minute repairs?

Ig-glue.

Where do Santa's helpers go to work out their problems?

An elf-help group.

What's an elf's favourite dog breed?

Toy poodle.

Santa's slick sleigh slides slightly on slick snow.

Tiny Timmy trims the tall tree with tons of tinsel.

What did the snowman say to the aggressive carrot?

'Get out of my face.'

REINDEER RUCKUS

What do you call a reindeer with three eyes?

A reiiindeer.

Why did Rudolph have to attend summer school?

Because he went down in history.

Which of Santa's reindeer is the fastest?

Dasher.

What do you call a reindeer ghost?

Cari-boo!

Why do reindeer like Beyoncé so much?

She sleighs.

What game do reindeer play at sleepovers?

Truth or deer.

What does Rudolph want for Christmas?

A Pony sleigh station.

What do reindeer say before they tell you a joke?

'This one's going to sleigh you.'

How does Rudolph know when Christmas is coming?

He refers to his calen-deer.

Why do Donner and Blitzen get to take so many coffee breaks?

Because they are Santa's star bucks.

What does Santa do when the reindeer drive too fast?

He holds on for deer life.

Which of Santa's reindeer has the best moves?

Dancer.

What do the reindeer say to Santa on Christmas Eve?

'We're ready to sleigh.'

Why does Scrooge love Rudolph the Red-Nosed Reindeer?

Because every buck is deer to him.

Where do Santa's reindeer stop for coffee?

Star-bucks.

What do reindeer hang on their tree?

Horna-ments.

What do you call an obnoxious reindeer?

Rude-olph.

Who did the reindeer invite to his Christmas party?

His nearest and deer-est friends.

Why is Rudolph so good at answering trivia questions?

He nose a lot.

Where will you find Santa's nine reindeer?

It depends where you left them.

Which of Santa's reindeer can you see from outer space?

Comet.

Why did no one bid for Rudolph and Blitzen on eBay?

Because they were too deer.

What do you call a blind reindeer?

No eye deer.

Where did Rudolph go to school?

He didn't, he was elf-taught.

Where does Rudolph go when he loses his tail?

Any good re-tailer.

Which of Santa's reindeer can be seen on Valentine's Day?

Cupid.

What do you call Santa's reindeer when they land in the Sahara Desert?

Lost.

Are Dancer and Prancer related?

No, but they are deer friends.

Which Elton John song best describes one of Santa's reindeer?

'Tiny Dancer'

Why does Mrs Claus always hug the reindeer?

They are so deer to her.

How many deer would a reindeer rein if a reindeer could rein deer?

Jolly Jack Frost jumped joyfully in the jingle bells.

Why couldn't the pony sing a lullaby?

She was a little horse.

CHRISTMAS CRAZIES

What is every parent's favourite Christmas song?

'Silent Night'

Why did the scarecrow get a big Christmas bonus?

He was outstanding in his field.

What happens if you eat Christmas decorations?

You get tinsilitis.

What do grapes sing at Christmas?

"Tis the season to be jelly'

What's the difference between the Christmas alphabet and the ordinary alphabet?

The Christmas alphabet has Noel.

What did the gingerbread man put on his bed?

A baking sheet.

Who is never hungry at Christmas?

The turkey - he's always stuffed.

What's the weather report every Christmas Eve?

There's 100% chance of reindeer.

How does the snow globe feel this year?

A little shaken.

What kind of bug hates Christmas?

A humbug.

What's red, white and blue at Christmas?

A sad candy cane.

What did the judge say to the angry Advent calendar?

'Your days are numbered!'

What did the bald man say when he got a comb for Christmas?

'I'll never part with it.'

What kind of Christmas carol do you sing to fruit?

'We Wish You a Berry Christmas'

What body part do you only see at Christmas?

The mistle-toe.

How did Scrooge win the football game?

The ghost of Christmas passed.

What's the best Christmas present?

A broken drum – you just can't beat it.

What do gingerbread men use when they break a leg?

A candy cane.

Why is a foot a good Christmas present?

It makes a good stocking filler.

What falls at the North Pole but never gets hurt?

Snow.

What is a vegan's favourite Christmas carol?

'Soy to the World'

Why is it so cold at Christmas in the Northern Hemisphere?

Because it's in Decemberrrrr.

What happened to the woman who stole an Advent calendar?

She got 25 days.

Why did the gingerbread man go to the doctor?

He was feeling crumby.

What instrument do monkeys play at Christmas?

Jungle bells.

Why did Santa go to music lessons?

He wanted to improve his wrapping skills.

In what year does New Year's Day come before Christmas?

Every year.

What do road crews use at the North Pole?

Snow cones.

What comes at the end of Christmas?

The letter S.

How does Darth Vader enjoy his Christmas turkey?

On the dark side.

Why didn't the skeleton go to the Christmas party?

He had no body to go with.

What do you use to decorate a canoe for Christmas?

Oar-naments.

Why do mummies like Christmas so much?

Because of all the wrapping.

If athletes get athlete's foot, what do astronauts get?

Missile-toe.

Why couldn't the teacher find anyone to help her wrap gifts?

No one was present.

What do you get when you cross an archer with a gift wrapper?

Ribbon Hood.

What's the best thing to put into a Christmas cake?

Your teeth.

What did the mum say to her kids after they opened their presents?

'What a Christmess.'

Why did Jimmy's school marks drop after the Christmas holidays?

Because everything was marked down.

What do you drain your Christmas cranberries with?

An Advent colander.

What is the most festive herb?

Christmas thyme.

What did the salt say to the pepper on Christmas Day?

'Seasonings Greetings!'

Where does Christmas come before Thanksgiving?

In the dictionary.

Why didn't the stocking eat Christmas dinner?

It was stuffed.

What is a maths teacher's favourite Christmas food?

Mince Pi.

Which year do Christmas Day and New Year's Day come in the same year?

Every year.

What is the most festive sea creature?

The Ru-dolphin.

Where do the best American Christmas singers live?

North Carol-ina.

What two things do kids want in December?

Their two front teeth.

What is a farmer's favourite Christmas carol?

'I'm Dreaming of a Wheat Christmas.'

Why do you go to bed on Christmas Eve?

Because the bed won't come to you.

What is Santa's favourite musical instrument?

The sleigh bell.

What bites but doesn't have any teeth?

Frost.

Which food will make you cry at Christmas?

An onion.

What's the hardest thing about learning to skate at the North Pole?

The ice.

Where does Frosty the Snowman keep his money?

In a snowbank.

Why does Santa's sled get such good mileage?

It has long-distance runners on each side.

What kind of egg can you drink?

Eggnog.

What do you have in December that you don't have in any other month?

The letter D.

Who hides in a bakery at Christmas?

A mince spy.

How do you find Will Smith in the snow?

Look for the fresh prints.

What did the snowflake say to the fallen leaf?

'You are so last season.'

How does Christmas Day begin?

With the letter C.

How does Christmas Day end?

With the letter Y.

Why did the gingerbread man go to school?

He wanted to be a smart cookie.

How does Santa take photos?

With a Pole-aroid camera.

If seven silly Santas sang sixteen silly songs, how many silly songs did seven silly Santas sing?

Five fluffy reindeer frolicked by the fireplace.

What does a cloud wear under its coat?

Thunderwear.

TREE TALES

What is as big as a Christmas tree but lighter than a feather?

Its shadow.

What did the Christmas tree do after its bank closed?

It started his own branch.

How do Christmas trees get their email?

They log on.

Why did the Christmas tree go to the dentist?

It needed a root canal.

What did Luke Skywalker say after he planted a Christmas tree farm?

'May the forest be with you.'

How did the two rival Christmas trees get along?

They signed a peace tree-ty.

What did one Christmas tree say to another?

'Lighten up.'

How do Christmas trees get ready for a night out?

They spruce up.

What is a Christmas tree's favourite shape?

A tree-angle.

What do you call cutting down a Christmas tree?

Christmas chopping.

Who is a Christmas tree's favourite singer?

Spruce Springsteen.

What did the beaver say to the Christmas tree?

'Nice gnawing you.'

Why did the Christmas tree go to the barber?

It needed a trim.

What month does a Christmas tree hate the most?

Sep-timber.

What do you get if you cross a Christmas tree with an apple?

A pine-apple.

Why wouldn't the Christmas tree stand up?

Because it has no legs.

What should you sing to a Christmas tree at its retirement party?

'Fir he's a jolly good fellow, fir he's a jolly good fellow . . .'

Why are Christmas trees so fond of the past?

The present's beneath them.

What is a Christmas tree's favourite candy?

Orna-mints.

Why are Christmas trees bad at sewing?

Because they always drop their needles.

What do you get when you wrap a Christmas tree with bacon?

A pork-u-pine.

What do you call a group of Christmas trees?

A forest of festivity.

What did Taylor Swift say to the Christmas tree when it got covered in too much snow?

'Shake it off.'

Where do little trees go to become Christmas trees?

Elementree school.

Why aren't animals afraid of Christmas trees?

They're all bark and no bite.

What did the Christmas tree say to the ornament?

'Aren't you tired of hanging around?'

Which winter sport do Christmas trees participate in?

Al-pine skiing.

What do scientists decorate at Christmas?

A chemis-tree.

What do Christmas trees wear to stay warm at the North Pole?

Fir coats.

How do Christmas trees keep their breath fresh?

They suck on an orna-mint.

Holly hangs holly
here hoping happy
holidays hurry.

Wobbly wreaths
wiggled wildly in
the winter wind.

What did one toilet say to the other?

You look flushed.

ANIMAL ANTICS

What's green, covered in Christmas lights and goes *ribbet ribbet*?

Mistle-toad.

How do sheep say Merry Christmas to each other?

'Fleece Navidad.'

What do you call a cat sitting on the beach on Christmas Eve?

Sandy Claws.

What did the grumpy sheep say when his friends wished him a happy Christmas?

'Baaaa humbug.'

Why did the turkey join the Christmas band?

Because he had the drumsticks.

Where do polar bears vote?

The North Poll.

What does a snake sing at Christmas?

'SSSsssssssssssssilent Night'

Who delivers Christmas presents to cats?

Santa Claws.

What do you give an artistic dog for Christmas?

A Fetch-A-Sketch.

What do fish sing at Christmas time?

Christmas corals.

How do sheep wish each other happy holidays?

'Merry Christmas to ewe!'

Which Christmas carol do dogs like best?

'Bark the Herald Angels Sing'

Who brings Christmas presents to fleas?

Old Saint Tick.

What did the cow get for Christmas?

A cowculator.

What do Christmas and crabs have in common?

Sandy claws.

Who delivers Christmas presents to dogs?

Santa Paws.

What do you call a litter of puppies born at the North Pole?

Santa's little yelpers.

What is a dog's favourite Christmas song?

'Fleas Navidad'

Blitzer bobbles a
billion brilliant bells.

Chilly chipper children cheerfully chant.

Why are balloons so expensive?
Because of inflation.

FROSTY FUN

What do snowmen sing at birthday parties?

'Freeze a Jolly Good Fellow.'

Why does everyone love Frosty the Snowman?

He's cool.

What is it called when a snowman has a temper tantrum?

A meltdown.

What do you call a snowman with a six-pack?

The abdominal snowman.

What do snowmen eat for lunch?

Icebergers.

What are the offspring of snowmen called?

Chill-dren.

How does a snowman lose weight?

He waits for the weather to get warmer.

What did one snowman say to the other snowman?

'Do you smell carrots?'

What do you get when you cross a snowman with a vampire?

Frostbite.

What do snowmen like most about school?

Snow and Tell.

Where do snowmen go to dance?

The snowball.

What do you call a snowman in the summer?

A puddle.

What did one snowman do to the other snowman when he was upset with him?

Gave him the cold shoulder.

How do you scare a snowman?

Turn on a hairdryer.

What do snowmen eat for breakfast?

Ice Bubbles.

What do you call an old snowman?

Water.

Why was the snowman looking through the pile of carrots?

He was picking his nose.

Why did the snowman go to school?

To become brrrighter.

Kris Kringle crunches candy canes.

Comet cuddles cute Christmas kittens carefully.

What do you call a pig that knows karate?

Pork chop.

SANTA SILLIES

What do you call Santa when he stops moving?

Santa Pause.

What does Santa suffer from if he gets stuck in a chimney?

Claus-trophobia.

Where do Santa's elves go swimming?

The North Pool.

How do you hire Santa Claus?

Put him on a ladder.

What kind of motorcycle does Santa drive?

A Holly Davidson.

Why does Santa have three gardens?

So he can ho, ho, ho.

What did Santa bring the football announcer who made the naughty list?

COOOOOOOAAAALLLLLLLL!

Why does Santa go down the chimney?

Because it soots him.

What did the English teacher call Santa's helpers?

Subordinate Clauses.

Which of Santa's friends is the most chill?

Jack Frost.

What's red and white and falls down chimneys?

Santa Clutz.

How can Santa deliver presents during a thunderstorm?

His sleigh is flown by rain-deer.

What's Santa's favourite type of potato chip?

Crisp Pringles.

What did Santa say when he stepped into a big puddle?

'It must have reind'eer.'

What is Santa's first language?

North Polish.

What is Santa's favourite kind of candy?

Jolly Ranchers.

How do you know when Santa's around?

You can sense his presents.

What was Santa's favourite subject in school?

Chemis-tree.

What is Santa's dog's name?

Santa Paws.

How much did Santa pay for his sleigh?

Nothing, it was on the house.

Which two letters describe Santa's sack after Christmas?

M.T.

What do you call a broke Santa Claus?

Saint-nickel-less.

What goes *oh, oh, oh?*

Santa walking backwards.

What did Santa's elves call him when he stepped on a bag of cashews?

A nutcracker.

What do you get if you cross Santa with a duck?

A Christmas quacker.

Why did Santa Claus get a parking ticket on Christmas Eve?

He left his sleigh in a snow parking zone.

Where does Santa go when Christmas is over?

On holiday to a ho-ho-ho-tel.

Why doesn't Santa go to the hospital?

He doesn't have elf care.

What did Santa's dog ask for this Christmas?

A mobile bone.

What smells the most in Santa's sleigh?

His nose.

Who is Santa's favourite singer?

Beyon-sleigh.

Why doesn't Santa eat junk food?

Because it's bad for his elf.

What do you get when Santa becomes a detective?

Santa Clues.

Why does Santa work at the North Pole?

Because the penguins kicked him out of the South Pole.

Do you know the kid who was scared of Santa?

He was Claus-trophobic.

What is Santa's favourite place to give presents in America?

Idaho-ho-ho.

Who is Santa's second favourite singer?

Elfish Presley.

What did Santa name his pet frog?

Mistletoad.

What do you call Santa when he goes down a chimney with a fire at the bottom?

Krisp Cringle.

What did Santa say at the start of the race?

'Ready, set, ho ho ho!'

Who delivers presents to baby sharks?

Santa Jaws.

Between Snoop Dog, Eminem and Dr Dre, who is Santa's favourite?

He can't choose. They're all good wrappers.

Why is Santa so good at karate?

Because he has a black belt.

What is Santa's favourite sandwich?

Peanut butter with jolly.

Where does Santa put his suit after Christmas?

In his Claus-et.

What did Santa say when he arrived back home?

'There's snow place like home.'

Where did Santa Claus go on holiday?

Santa Cruz.

What is Santa's mum's name?

Mary Christmas.

What goes *ho, ho, whoosh, ho, ho, whoosh*?

Santa sweeping the floor.

What is red and white, red and white, and red and white again?

Santa Claus rolling down a hill.

What do a Christmas tree and Santa's beard have in common?

They both need trimming.

If you are related to Mr and Mrs Claus, what is your relation?

A relative clause.

What reaction do you get if Santa likes your dance performance?

Santapplause.

What is Santa's tax status?

Elf-employed.

What did the sea say to Santa?

Nothing. It just waved.

Did you hear about the invisible Santa?

You can't see him, but you can feel his presents.

Why does Santa work only one day a year?

There is a Claus in his contract.

What does Santa put on his toast?

Jingle jam.

What smells the most in a chimney on Christmas Eve?

Santa's nose.

What does Santa eat for breakfast?

Mistle-toast.

Frosty the snowman
slipped on slippery ice.

Eleven elves licked eleven little liquorice lollipops.

What has four wheels and flies?

A garbage truck.

RIDDLE ME THIS . . . CHRISTMAS

I'm a Christmas treat that can be made into many things. I can be a cake, a cookie or even a house. What am I?

Gingerbread.

I have needles all over me, but I cannot sew a thing. What am I?

A Christmas tree.

I'm at every house Santa visits and when he finds me, he knows he's in for a treat. What am I?

Milk and cookies.

All day I sit on a shelf, but I come alive and move during the night. I tell Santa who's been naughty and who's been nice. Who am I?

The Elf on the Shelf.

I can travel all around the world just like Santa Claus, but I never leave my corner. What am I?

A stamp.

I have many keys, but I can't open Santa's sleigh. What am I?

A piano.

I'm a bank, but I don't have any money. What am I?

A snowbank.

My body is round, with a carrot for a nose. I love to be cold, from my head to my toes. What am I?

A snowman.

Normally you find me on people's feet, but during Christmas I hang from fireplaces. What am I?

Stockings.

I'm grumpy and green and stole Christmas one night. But then my heart grew, and I set it all right. Who am I?

The Grinch.

I am tall when I am young, and I am short when I am old. What am I?

A Christmas candle.

I have many colours all shiny and bright, I turn houses into a beautiful sight. What am I?

Christmas lights.

I come in two different colours and am minty and sweet. You'll be hooked on me – isn't that neat? What am I?

A candy cane.

I keep gifts safe for people all around the world. What am I?

A Christmas tree.

I am a shape. I am a fish.
I am part of the sky.
You'll find me on the top
of a Christmas tree.
What am I?

A star.

If Santa's five elves take five minutes to make five dolls, how long would it take 100 elves to make 100 dolls?

Five minutes.

If you look up at Christmas, you will see me hanging above. People stand beneath me and kiss someone they love.
What am I?

Mistletoe.

I'm a catchy carol and a tune that likes to rhyme, I contain 12 special gifts that come around Christmas time.
What am I?

'The Twelve Days of Christmas'

Making everything white is my aim. No two pieces of me are ever the same. Playing with me is everyone's favourite winter game. What am I?

Snow.

I am a ball that does not bounce. What am I?

A snowball.

Santa's sack stuffed
with silly surprises.

Prancer presents pumpkin pies and presents.

What do you call a sleeping bull?

A bulldozer.

KNOCK KNOCK IT'S CHRISTMAS!

Knock, knock.
Who's there?
Mary.
Mary who?
Mary Christmas.

Knock, knock.
Who's there?
Dewey.
Dewey who?
Dewey know how long it is until Santa gets here?

Knock, knock.
Who's there?
Wayne.
Wayne who?
Wayne in a manger.

Knock, knock.
Who's there?
Noah.
Noah who?
Noah good Christmas joke?

Knock, knock.
Who's there?
Chris.
Chris who?
Christmas is here!

Knock, knock.
Who's there?
Olive.
Olive who?
Olive Christmastime, don't you?

Knock, knock.
Who's there?
Coal.
Coal who?
Coal me when Santa's on his way.

Knock, knock.
Who's there?
Dexter.
Dexter who?
Dexter halls with boughs of holly . . .

Knock, knock.
Who's there?
Avery.
Avery who?
Avery Merry Christmas to you.

Knock, knock.
Who's there?
Santa.
Santa who?
Santa Christmas card to you, did you get it?

Knock, knock.
Who's there?
Elf.
Elf who?
Elf me wrap this present for Santa.

Knock, knock.
Who's there?
Holly.
Holly who?
Holly-days are here again.

Knock, knock.
Who's there?
Interrupting Santa.
Inter–
Ho, ho, ho! Merry Christmas!

Knock, knock.
Who's there?
Anna.
Anna who?
Anna partridge in a pear tree.

Knock, knock.
Who's there?
Tree.
Tree who?
Tree wise men.

Knock, knock.
Who's there?
Freeze!
Freeze who?
Freeze a jolly good fellow.

Knock, knock.
Who's there?
Pikachu.
Pikachu who?
Pikachu Christmas presents and you'll be in trouble.

Knock, knock.
Who's there?
Gladys.
Gladys who?
Gladys Christmas, aren't you?

Knock, knock.
Who's there?
Ho Ho.
Ho Ho who?
Your Santa impression needs a little work.

Knock, knock.
Who's there?
Ya.
Ya who?
Wow, you're really excited about Christmas!

Knock, knock.
Who's there?
Justin.
Justin who?
Justin time for Christmas cookies.

Knock, knock.
Who's there?
Doughnut.
Doughnut who?
Doughnut open until Christmas!

Knock, knock.
Who's there?
Charlotte.
Charlotte who?
Charlotte of fun to be had at Christmas.

Knock, knock.
Who's there?
Pudding.
Pudding who?
Pudding up the Christmas lights.

Knock, knock.
Who's there?
Howard.
Howard who?
Howard you like to sing Christmas carols with me?

Knock, knock.
Who's there?
Norway.
Norway who?
Norway am I kissing anyone under the mistletoe!

Knock, knock.
Who's there?
Yule.
Yule who?
Yule never guess.

Knock, knock.

Who's there?

Harry.

Harry who?

Harry up and open your present!

Knock, knock.

Who's there?

Snow.

Snow who?

Snow time like Christmas time.

Knock, knock.

Who's there?

Luke.

Luke who?

Luke at all those presents!

Knock, knock.
Who's there?
Candy.
Candy who?
Candy Christmas tree fit any more gifts under it?

Knock, knock.
Who's there?
Otis.
Otis who?
O'tis the season to be jolly, fa-la-la-la-la, la-la-la-la!

Knock, knock.

Who's there?

Snow.

Snow who?

Snow use. I have forgotten my name again.

Knock, knock.

Who's there?

Honda.

Honda who?

Honda first day of Christmas, my true love gave to me . . .

Pretty packages perfectly packed in paper.

Santa secretly sips sugary syrup.

What do librarians take when they go fishing?

Book worms.

Q&A WITH SANTA

Q: Do you have a middle name?

A: I do! But I like to keep it a secret. I can tell you that it begins with W. Can you guess what it is?

Q: How do you deliver presents to all the kids around the world in one night?

A: I have a magical sleigh, pulled by my crack team of highly trained reindeer who can fly really fast. I also have a special map that helps me plan the best route to make sure I get to visit all the homes around the world.

Q: How do you fit all the presents into your sleigh?

A: My elves have a special magic that comes to life every Christmas Eve that helps them fit all the gifts perfectly in my sleigh. It's like a giant puzzle!

Q: How do you fit down a chimney with that big belly of yours?

A: I have a special Santa trick that lets me shrink myself to fit through any chimney.

Q: But what about all the homes that don't have a chimney?

A: After all these years of visiting children on Christmas Eve, I know all the ways to find my way to the Christmas tree.

Q: What is your favourite food?

A: Well, for 364 days of the year I try to eat well and not over indulge. But it's the opposite on Christmas Eve! Children leave me all sorts of yummy treats, but my favourite is a very large chocolate chip cookie.

Q: Do you have a special Christmas Eve playlist?

A: Well, this probably won't surprise you, but I do tend to listen to 'Santa Claus is Coming to Town' on repeat, until Rudolph protests and we have to put his special song on repeat.

Q: How do you keep track of your Naughty or Nice lists for so many kids around the world?

I will let you in on a secret: Mrs Claus and our clever elves help me manage that. They keep me up to date on who has been naughty and who has been nice!

Q: How do you stay quiet while delivering presents?

A: My boots are made with special padding that helps me move silently on any surface. It's like tiptoeing on clouds!

Q: Who brings *you* gifts for Christmas?

A: Ho, ho, ho, that's a great question! When I come back to the North Pole after delivering all the gifts to the children of the world, there is always something lovely waiting for me. And I have never discovered who leaves it for me!

Q: Who is the hardest working elf?

A: Not the one on the shelf!

Q: What's the best part about your job?

A: I get to see the world from up above, and I can always spot the best places to land and deliver presents.

Crazy kids clamour
for candy canes and
Christmas cookies.

Santa stuffs Stephie's striped stocking.

What side of a turkey has the most feathers?

The outside.

Q&A WITH RUDOLPH

Q: How do you motivate the team to stay in shape all year round when they only get to perform to their peak ability one day of the year?

A: It's a full-time job! We train every day - distance running, interval sprints, take-offs and landings. We also make sure we carb-load all through December so we peak exactly at sunset on 24 December each year. But Mrs Claus keeps us well fed and looked after. That, and knowing how happy we make kids, is enough motivation for us!

Q: How do you keep your nose so bright?

A: Good genetics, mostly. But I also eat a lot of sparkly snowflakes, and on Christmas Eve, Mrs Claus makes me a special glow-in-the-dark smoothie to make sure my nose doesn't dim.

Q: How did you become Santa's lead reindeer?

A: You've probably heard the story, but . . .
It was a foggy Christmas Eve and Santa got lost on his way to visit the children in Liechtenstein for the third year in a row. Apparently he'd heard a rumour about my bright, shiny nose, so suddenly out of nowhere he appeared and asked me a big favour . . . and ever since then, I get to lead the reindeer all over the world. Those couple of nasty reindeer don't give me grief anymore.

Q: Does Santa have any bad habits?

A: Well, let's just say he could bring us back a few more cookies from his visits.

Q: What is your favourite Christmas song?

A: I'll give you three guesses.

Q: What's your favourite holiday treat?

A: Carrot cake! Mrs Claus makes a special one for each of us on Christmas Eve.

Q: What do you do when you're not helping Santa on Christmas Eve?

A: I love playing hide-and-seek in the snow with my reindeer friends. My glowing nose makes it more of a challenge!

Q: Do you have any tips for kids who feel a bit different, like you once were?

A: Embrace your unique talents - everyone has something that makes them special. Lots of reindeer thought my bright red nose was capital-w Weird, but look how that turned out. Be proud of who you are and never be afraid to stand out in a crowd.

Seven Santas sang
silly songs.

Ten tiny tin trains
toot ten times.

What is a witch's favourite subject at school?

Spelling.

CHRISTMAS QUIZ

1: What is the date of Christmas Day?

A) 24 December

B) 25 December

C) 31 December

2: What other names does Santa Claus go by?

3: Where does Santa Claus live?

4: Who helps Santa make all the toys to deliver to children on Christmas Eve?

5: What kind of houses are popular to make and decorate at Christmas time?

6: How many times does Santa check his list to determine who is naughty and who is nice?

7: What do people traditionally decorate during Christmas?

A) Easter eggs

B) Christmas tree

C) Birthday cake

8: Which reindeer has a red nose?

9: Can you name all of Santa's reindeer?

10: What do people hang by the fireplace during Christmas?

A) Stockings

B) Socks

C) Mittens

11: What is the name of the famous reindeer with a shiny nose?

12: What colour is Santa's suit?

There's chimney soot on Santa's suit.

Ten tiny toy soldiers tinker with twenty toy trains.

Why did the boy sprinkle sugar on his pillow?

He wanted to have sweet dreams.

CHRISTMAS CROSSWORDS

CHRISTMAS TREATS

Down:

1. What slice is made from Rice Bubbles, coconut and other sweet things and belongs on your Christmas table?
2. What is a creamy, rich drink often enjoyed at Christmas?
4. Which cold layered dessert might you see on the table on Christmas Day?
5. What is a delicious warm drink made from milk and chocolate and often topped with marshmallows?

Across:

3. What is a yummy snack that can be made into a person or a house – or anything Christmassy?
6. What is a traditional cake people eat at Christmastime? (Hint: It contains fruit!)
7. What kind of pudding is eaten after Christmas lunch or dinner?
8. What is Santa's favourite treat that is shaped like a cane?
9. What is a special dessert made with meringue and cream that people love to eat on Christmas Day?

ELVES

Down:

1. What is the busiest month of the year for Santa's elves?
2. What is a toy/vehicle the elves make for kids each Christmas?
5. What shape are the shoes worn by Santa's elves?
7. What are Santa's little helpers called?
8. What animal stands guard outside Santa's workshop?
9. What language do elves speak?

Across:

3. What is a toy the elves make for babies each Christmas?
4. What sound do elves make when they laugh?
6. Which animal is an elf's favourite?
10. Where do Santa's elves make all the toys for children? Santa's --------?
11. What helps the elves make all the toys in time for Christmas each year?
12. What is a tool the elves use in their workshop?

WINTER CHRISTMAS

Down:

1. Something to wrap around your neck to stay warm.
3. Santa gets one of these every Christmas Eve – if you're lucky, you might get one in December!
4. Swap your shoes for these to glide around on a frozen lake or at a rink.
5. How's the weather for a white Christmas?

Across:

2. These will keep your hands warm – you'll need a pair when you step outside.
6. This crackles and glows and warms you up if you stand close to it.
7. A sweet drink that will warm you inside.
8. The best kind of outdoor 'fight' where nobody gets hurt.
9. Something white and fun that sprinkles down and can be made into a man.
10. You'll need this when you go outside.

SUMMER CHRISTMAS

Down:

1. Cooks sausages for a park picnic.
2. Where the waves meet the sand.
3. Something you experience a lot in Australia all through December.
4. An Aussie dessert made of meringue, cream and fruit.
7. Icy cold treats on a stick you can enjoy/slurp at the beach.

Across:

5. A game often played by families on Christmas Day. You'll need a bat, ball and wickets.
6. Something you might eat at Christmas lunch if you don't like roast turkey.
8. Your favourite people to spend Christmas with.
9. What Santa rides to deliver presents to the beach.
10. What to do after lunch on 25 December.

CHRISTMAS CRAZINESS

Down:

1. What is a popular Christmas song '------ Bells'?
2. What hangs on a Christmas tree?
3. What is a sweet drink made from cocoa and topped with marshmallows?
5. What is the colour of Rudolph's nose?
8. What gives you a small gift each day leading up to Christmas?
11. What is a frozen treat made of milk and sugar?

Across:

4. What is a popular Christmas story about a grumpy green character?
6. What is the name of the most famous reindeer?
7. What is the name of a famous, jolly old man who delivers presents once a year?
9. Who helps Santa make all the gifts for children?
10. What is Santa's favourite Christmas Eve treat (that goes perfectly with milk)?

REINDEER RECOLLECTION

Down:

2. Which reindeer can be a bit of a show-off?

5. Which reindeer is the first on the dance floor?

6. Which reindeer has an interest in astronomy?

8. Which reindeer always comes last in the alphabet?

Across:

1. Which is the most famous reindeer of all?

3. Which reindeer is dashingly handsome?

4. Which reindeer is popular on Valentine's Day?

7. Which reindeer is named after thunder?

9. Which reindeer is super-fast?

SUPER SANTA

Down:

2. What is a sweet treat Santa likes to eat on Christmas Eve?
4. What kind of facial hair does Santa have?
7. Who are the magical creatures who help Santa make toys?
8. What colour are Santa's boots?
9. What is one of Santa's nicknames?
12. How does Santa travel around the world on Christmas Eve?

Across:

1. What is the name of Santa's wife?
3. Where does Santa live?
5. What colour is Santa's suit?
6. What month is Santa's birthday?
10. How many reindeer pull Santa's sleigh?
11. What are the two lists Santa keeps for children during the year? Naughty and –?
13. Who is the jolly man who delivers presents on Christmas Eve?
14. What happy sound does Santa make as he pops down a chimney?

CHRISTMAS GIFTS

Down:

1. What kind of car do kids love to get for Christmas?
3. What's a cool 1980s toy that spins on a string?
4. What is Santa's favourite gift to receive from the North Pole Bakery?
6. What is something you can wave around to make bubbly fun fly around?
9. What is a popular toy made of bricks that can be stuck together to make new things?

Across:

2. What is a soft, cuddly present you could give a baby?
5. What is a gift Santa brings to kids who like to kick things on a field?
7. What's a toy Santa brings that you can ride that's not a bicycle?
8. What is a special toy that Santa often brings to little kids to play with?
10. What is a gift that can be enjoyed again and again?

Tinsel tangled terribly on the towering tree.

Gingerbread giggled while getting glittered.

What do frogs wear on their feet?

Open toad sandals.

FIND THESE
FESTIVE WORDS

SUMMER CHRISTMAS

H I Y C Y I C Y P O L E S I D G O F R H
O I C V F A V W J I Q H O C S W I Z F P
L H Q E O R S E B A R B E C U E M E N Q
I L R A C W I Q X V M I K Z B S A Y Y L
D Q H S T R J S A J X S U N S C R E E N
A Z P C E P E J B M D N O Q L Q Q J F I
Y I I S B A D A U E P A E R O E X Q I U
S A C U E U S J M Q E I Q Y Z F O Z R N
Y I N N A Y U H P Y V K T A H P I R E L
I A I K C D D P E E M B Z W E O T Q W Q
N B C E H S U N G L A S S E S X U B O H
N H I B Q Z R D A L L S U R F B O A R D
W A T E R M E L O N Z S J S N U A S K D
O N K P H M M Y L T J D Z G E V M Y S N
A A L E M O N A D E S A N D C A S T L E
V N Y E O V T N J J Z J E F G I G Y M M
V R A E D M B N T H C U N X D O J U U N
K W D P J M W C P S W I M M I N G P L M
V A T Y C G F G V U A B Z T M P T D H L
K N D P L K I R G S T N I I T P O J V Y

sandcastle
surfboard
seashells
lemonade
holidays
picnic

watermelon
sunscreen
fireworks
barbecue
seagull
beach

sunglasses
ice cream
icy poles
swimming
frisbee
sun

CHRISTMAS FOOD

```
Q Z N Z W N V X P C W X C T O X N S R E
E F K C A N D Y C A N E S K J A Q C D G
G D U C R O A S T T U R K E Y N P R U G
F R I J P B N O S P M W M Q B V G A L N
G L Q Q F N C O U F L G E V Z G P N T O
S T U F F I N G W U K O U J H R S B J G
A E E E W U T P C U K J L L S U F E P Q
K V F H R L D R I P L J O L B T E R A Z
S I G E N P I Y N E T Y P F I T M R S L
D K G J F R U I T C A K E K E E N Y P E
L P X R A U D G Y R X I S H A P S S R K
K K A Y A H O T C H O C O L A T E A A N
I O O V T V R F Q E V U H C O M G U W S
R C X D L J Y V Z G B Y R Q L L I C N J
T U S I O O D R B F M X X G M O W E S Y
W G G X N T V G W K T U E D X X O J L C
X W L W U X N A N E R X M D G C A T U N
C W H I T E C H R I S T M A S K O X P K
H V O B Y W K T J G A A X A X I R K N J
H B Y G I N G E R B R E A D H O U S E Q
```

gingerbread house	candy canes	gravy
white christmas	stuffing	lollies
cranberry sauce	pavlova	eggnog
hot chocolate	prawns	ham
roast turkey	fruitcake	

CHRISTMAS

P D E T I S Z C A N D Y C A N E S B H S
M F X E N B C O Q D D Y W E O S S Z Q T
F F A Q G B G Z T M C H R A M L N D D O
E Q S Z Z L R U K W N O B Y C E K J I C
V T E D C I R H W C A T G W T I C E U K
R X G C Q T E S K H R C S T I G H D J I
Q Z G K D Z J W K R B H S O N H R V W N
E X N C U E M X Z I Q O M C S R I L H G
C J O Q D N Z O I S Q C B A E I S J T S
V Z G W W J D D O T Z O O R L D T H S X
C G B V N X F F D M F L G O S E M O N K
B H Y J M Z J M L A R A P L M W A L O X
E J I C Y Z L B U S C T H S W W S L W T
S Z U M A C U F V P I E T H H S L Y F U
X L G F N B P Q J U F X D K Q X I B L G
A N H N O E Z Z P D F F F T H T G F A I
M V C R K Q Y N I D N J V U H A H B K F
F H D E C O R A T I O N S U K C T N E T
H R T G H B R H P N F A O F J T S Q S S
K X U D A K X V Z G M Q D E B B I V A H

christmas pudding	candy cane	carols
christmas lights	stockings	blitzen
hot chocolate	sleigh ride	eggnog
decorations	chimney	holly
snowflakes	tinsel	gifts

ELVES

P A X C C C P K T R A I N S V Z O F B G W Q E F Q P E W Q B
Y X U Q L E T F S B U I L D I N G B L O C K S D K R Y T C F
Q D B U X B S A P Q B A R M C G E P P C H M W Q N Q F D A Z
D B H I B N S M M C F X L F K Z Y K V D I S U H W U I G C K
E L D D K J P F G F O W D V Y B P B R C V A M H W H G H T A
R N G X I C T N E O X H P U M A U I I Z T N Z T U R G J B J
C V V F T X Y M T C Z N G Z G V O R N C F T Q T V H Y C K N
T L M V E A E L R T E R Z U X K F G D D Y A Q T R W U P U W
V X G X S H K W E S V I E A X X C R B G R C K D M R I O E R
B U O I U J J H A D C Y A P N I Y S F P F T L Z P A D L S I
R R Z C D J R D Z N Z L I P N M E D D N F H E E A F V O L F
Z U G E Y B Z F Z N P Z A L A A E E O W V B X B S T S J E J
K O A H G O D S P H Z X L U Z O A O L Q E H L I N G S A H G
C M L V I F Y V H Z I Q G B S L G M L D V S C C T O G E I S
C H Q N F I P O W O C D E X L U B J S F S Y D D I A Q V K Z
C I R G A R O K S E D O L S B N S P L N K D R B F R L A K V
M O C I I T O Q I R U G Q V U D M Z V C I Z B H J B F D L T
J H Q T S W M G U Q M K K H W J Q B N R P U N J C H O G Y V
E E P I H T F M D M Y V R G T C E N X W P N V S G W M O I R
Z A L S E C M E A C W G Y O H T K N G J I T N Q L B D Z K D
S Q C V Q I G A E W U H V C E S C L V T N M H P M V S O W S
K W P J E Z I G S R A N F V Q Q B P G A G S X F R W E W D G
T B X W S S Q X I E X M F O K X C V K A R P J F F W A R M E
K K X Y R T N Q U L V D Y C L A R C G E O K B X J R C D L B
W S A A T H N A M N P E Y I A R P I N Y P G A M E S U J E Y
H S I Q M X U E B J A B V U E V K Y M W E K R H G A M K D Y
Q B H P P Y S A A D D T M I U I S Q A Z P G I K U S M P H R
V L P O I N T Y H A T S G A N M P I D O R S O Q X G E C K H
N Y I V O I B U J C R Y N W O R K S H O P M U P A L R E A U
Q T D X Z C P U M N K A X Z X C T A C U Q N V Z W Q T J X A

building blocks	mrs claus	books
skipping rope	bicycles	yoyos
christmas eve	trains	dolls
pointy hats	elves	kites
workshop	santa	games

REINDEER

```
W L J F T U T F X P R P P K U I K I L E Q Y J V F U O D T V
F Q J N C K T U D V D U K J W D H R E O O Q S B D I A E Z O
C W Z Y Z L H S N R N P A J P Z L Y N M Y E O T F N G Y G Y
R V A Z X E S R I N D P P C G B B W B U U P W S C V A Y I V
E Y K Z D D T R G R D T T U L R K D W B O S Y C X I W M X A
D Q V J B G K B G Q Q O G P K Y T T M J R K A Q G X E C Q Y
N J Q E L K H X P Y M D C I R T W L G S G A R S J E L J O N
O N E D E J L G O R T X S D V Q Z A T H Y H Q B L N Z C G L
S O L J Z T R Q X N Q Z W D A N C E R U S A N A D K F G Q N
E R Y X K L E N G P G U D O N N E R E P N U R E I N D E E R
U T P W K Q J N U O Q W B L X Y A W H D O G L I P J L P U P
M H H P Z C U S Y S U V N L W U M W G Z W G H J Y W F Z F Q
W P C E O P I Y L X J O Z X A T Q L L T S F Y M U E O K Q D
M O D N V C R N J R J I L W S Q T U H J L H C T C P B V L B
K L R I W F C A D D S I P W R D B D G X F A N N V G H O P U
Y E X A J E E T N Q L A Z S E H F D K L D E G Z D R Z W D H
Y Y A S U B X W T C Z O N Q I S L E I G H V A J O M P V P F
O Y Y X C O M E T Y E C L T F M T E N X B O Z B N M N O U G
T K R I T Y E I L Q K R T X A X D K M Q E B N X Y B R I O I
A W D M B Z B E D N G A O R L D O M W L G K C J V Y B V L C
T C B Q S U B J A J P X K B U C J Z I A Z S N Z U L F I A S
G V L W M H R Q S D Y T D J J D H T H F O K S L K C B W A M
N K I Q V E X B H I S X R Q O K O D G D D L W A J J Q X R S
Q N T L P B H G E F X P C V L G K L J X I G E B T M Y O L U
G Y Z N Q G W K R T C S D M V J K W P T I O U A E L V Q T D
R F E A E Z N F N O O E K Y E Z Q E E H C R Z A D Y B P E Z
H F N W G B S G S P V U R U X D Y Z V F E F U S E J S N M T
M T T V J H H V Z X D F A Y A I Z V J I K T I K J F T F N L
E X X P D T C P T R Z O D Z H V P R P D S H O Y H J I W S A
R K T F Q U F Y B C Q L U I F O W A X B F U T Q G H E S Y T
```

north pole	red nose	vixen
reindeer	dasher	comet
prancer	dancer	cupid
blitzen	donner	santa
rudolph	sleigh	snow

MORE CHRISTMAS

```
G C X Q R H E L V E S T Z N S U L E G B X P Y P J J E A T I
V H B X V X L N P H R E F N A S Z Q I D J Q U K Q M F Y J H
I R Z T M N P M C Q F W H M U C I Z O C T M F R T A L Y V W
J I R P S A C I A Y P K U X R N D L H N N O R T H P O L E U
A S H H N M Q C L Q V L O D Q A H L I O X A R Y H T A S M S
T T G H I X R R N B E F J R K Q V U A N X M R S C L A U S N
M M M R B S G O F Y T U L E O R N A M E N T S B G G X Y Q O
D A L M S D W B F H S A M V W E G I I Q O U G W J H B R H W
G S I F P J L P O R H L X T R N Z T A T P S T O Y N X R M M
G B N T S L C D L Q V A D I U Z C I H T R S M R G N J K W A
C Z Y O K M G E X H I Q K L D J Z O Z W O E Y B L N I G S N
Q Y O O V Y W M F Q X V U Z O X U E Z U R F E A C B N U T F
U D W U I L B M J L D K Z O L R T P C Y N A I N D G G K J T
O W O E X Q E H V X Z F G S P R E E H B I H T S P H L E F T
U I W Q W L H S Y L A R H M H Q A H J P E E X M Y M E B E J
K U K C Z U U N L C G S J Y U V D S B J T A T Z N H B K N D
Q K D I D H L W N E E R G R W O R K S H O P Z J D P E U Z T
I I S U G Z T R N C I X O E F W T D O C S S J X P I L H Q Q
V L R M P Q B N K T T G V H G B K G M C H Q G E Z H L B M C
Y Y E Y D U T I F O G H H M W N P K U J K F W F J E S N K B
K V I T S J X A T C W N V K F N I D N Y B H J J B U L H K E
J R N I N K S L K A R N O I U Q J G K K A W V Q Z T L U V G
K H D R E E I A J M I S T L E T O E I J O K P V S X O A A P
S U E R Y P O I N M J J B P Y U W S Z W W T V J I D R Q R H
U P E Z V L R A L T M C I Q Q P X H K V T O W M J B A Z M R
P F R W K W A K A N A T O M B M D S P N N Y I C F Q R A D S
S E L L Q K S G D Q X X F L P A Z K Q V W S X J G V V P O Y
W B A A W N O K K O D I H C W U W R B O V P Z K B U Y W I C
K Z M B P V F D Z W H X T B Z C X H B P F T H J H T R L J J
D H Q X T W M G M I B Z V G A X J N X T I L I T L Q O U I N
```

jingle bells	reindeer	workshop
north pole	mrs claus	santa
ornaments	rudolph	elves
mistletoe	snowman	toys
christmas	sleigh	tree

SANTA

C	Y	B	C	J	V	O	N	I	C	E	L	I	S	T	I	S	Q	F	G
C	Y	V	J	R	D	T	M	H	O	H	O	H	O	Y	G	X	J	K	C
R	Z	M	O	E	F	A	T	H	E	R	C	H	R	I	S	T	M	A	S
C	U	I	L	D	L	Q	Q	S	B	V	F	X	V	M	N	H	V	H	B
Z	J	L	L	S	L	E	F	T	B	B	L	A	C	K	B	E	L	T	Z
P	Q	K	Y	U	C	A	F	T	I	K	J	N	Y	C	S	N	L	S	V
R	J	A	B	I	C	W	S	D	M	Q	B	V	F	X	Y	T	E	E	L
E	Z	N	Y	T	H	Y	J	H	J	L	G	C	S	O	K	U	X	K	R
S	W	D	U	L	R	L	N	F	U	M	G	H	B	Q	R	N	K	V	X
E	B	C	D	S	I	T	B	Y	G	H	D	Q	O	Y	E	F	R	V	N
N	H	O	T	I	S	K	O	I	C	G	K	C	P	M	F	H	I	T	V
T	P	O	H	M	T	M	V	K	R	A	K	W	S	U	J	R	S	U	A
S	C	K	L	X	M	W	S	A	N	T	A	C	L	A	U	S	K	O	E
V	C	I	R	S	A	I	N	T	N	I	C	H	O	L	A	S	R	F	K
R	M	E	G	I	S	W	F	J	V	O	B	J	H	S	L	E	I	G	H
E	T	S	C	O	E	M	R	S	C	L	A	U	S	D	P	K	N	J	E
G	J	G	G	F	V	F	G	W	J	O	C	A	H	W	W	X	G	X	Y
N	R	B	M	S	E	S	P	V	P	P	B	N	O	Q	R	R	L	F	I
F	C	U	G	F	L	U	R	X	B	M	B	S	B	S	Q	O	E	U	Y
Z	G	W	N	A	U	G	H	T	Y	L	I	S	T	F	B	B	Z	F	J

father christmas
milk and cookies
saint nicholas
naughty list
christmas eve

kris kringle
santa claus
black belt
mrs claus
nice list

sleigh
presents
ho ho ho
red suit
jolly

WINTER CHRISTMAS

A M Q N T V G I N G E R B R E A D Z T S
T O I C P J J P D N L F L R G V Z Y I B
Y R F Q W N W J T X O I J U Y D P F X Q
F R O S T Y T H E S N O W M A N D A L F
V G N T D D C A N D Y C A N E W U U F Y
Q S A N T A C L A U S X Z M G Z B E R A
N X X D C W X G J Z O Q G C H C F D R P
C G P T A I C H R I S T M A S T R E E E
H W Y I R C N V X J L U K V E Z F P F R
I I Y N O I S Q E R X B Z M Q B K R S E
M S A S L C U M Q I D O Q O F A I E T I
N U B E S L N J I N G L E B E L L S O N
E V U L Z E I S N O W F L A K E Q U C D
Y X W D M C B N P R E S E N T S K N K E
I H O T C H O C O L A T E X S P N U I E
U K Q N K X Q D H H S G S O U L E T N R
I E G X P Q A R H I H B Y X V C E H G A
H Q W S N O W M A N Q X R A D V H I S O
L K S F I J T W R E A T H Q N W J W G H
Z F M E B E C Y V W Q K A W A N A A V H

frosty the snowman
christmas tree
hot chocolate
jingle bells
santa claus
snowflake

candy cane
reindeer
presents
snowman
gingerbread
chimney

sleigh
wreath
stockings
icicle
tinsel
carols

Dear/Hello/Hi Santa,
This year I have been:

Dear/Hello/Hi Santa,

This year I have been:

- ☐ Really, really good all year.
- ☐ Pretty good most of the year.
- ☐ Good enough for enough of the year.

So, please could you put me on your Nice list?
(You can put my brother/sister/cousins
on the Naughty list.)

Here is a list of the things I would really like for Christmas, please! (I promise to leave you a yummy treat on Christmas Eve.)

....

....

....

Thank you, Santa.
You're the best!

From..

Dear/Hello/Hi Santa,
This year I have been:
Not super good, to be honest

Dear/Hello/Hi Santa,

This year I have been:

- ☐ Not super good, to be honest.
- ☐ Um, I could have cleaned up my room a bit more.
- ☐ Maybe let's not go into detail.

So, I know I'm probably on your Naughty list, but I think I deserve maybe just one present. Or two. If you could swing it, here are a few things that would MAKE MY CHRISTMAS. And I promise to be better next year!

....

....

....

Thank you, Santa.
You're the best!

From..

A is for . . .
Antlers
(Santa's reindeer have them!)

B is for . . .
Baking cookies
(choc-chip are best)

C is for . . .
Candy canes
(red and green, whichever you like)

D is for . . .
Dashing through the snow

E is for . . .
Elf on the Shelf
(Have you made the nice list?)

F is for . . .
Frosty the Snowman

G is for . . .
Gingerbread house
(or person or star or surfboard)

H is for . . .
Hot chocolate

I is for . . .
Icicles and ice cream
(depending on where you live)

J is for . . .
Jingle (all the way) bells

K is for . . .
Kris Kringle

L is for . . .
Light-hearted laughter

M is for . . .
Mistletoe
(but Mrs Claus might have something to say about that)

N is for . . .
the North Pole

O is for . . .
Ornaments

P is for . . .
Pyjamas all day because it's Christmas

Q is for . . .
Quirky gifts for/from your nanna

R is for . . .
Rudolph the Red-Nosed Reindeer

S is for . . .
Santa's sleigh

T is for . . .
Tinsel on the tree

U is for . . .
Ugly Christmas jumpers

V is for ...
Vixen pulling the sleigh

W is for ...
Wacky winter wonderland

X is for ...
Xtra special gifts

Y is for ...
You better watch out!

Z is for ...
Zany holiday traditions

ANSWERS

CHRISTMAS TREATS

ELVES

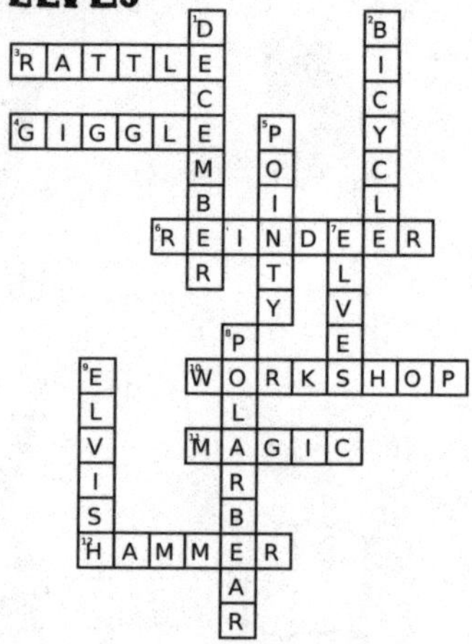

WINTER CHRISTMAS

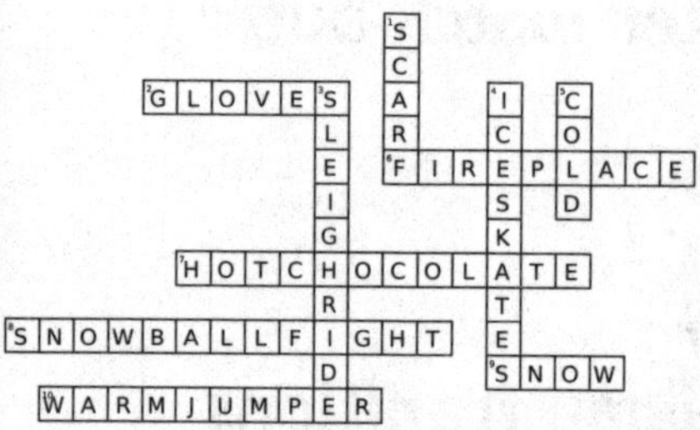

SUMMER CHRISTMAS

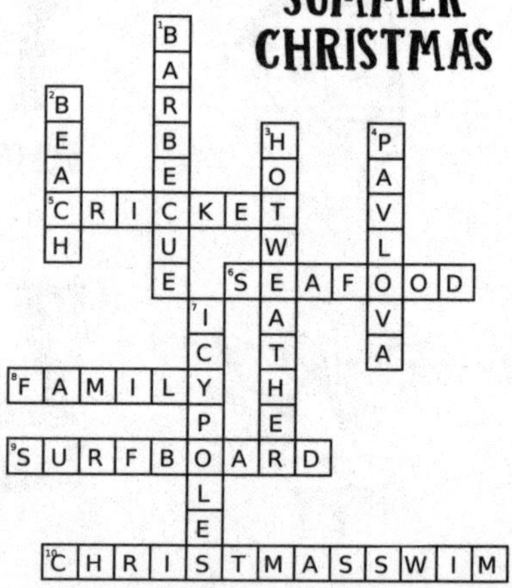

CHRISTMAS CRAZINESS

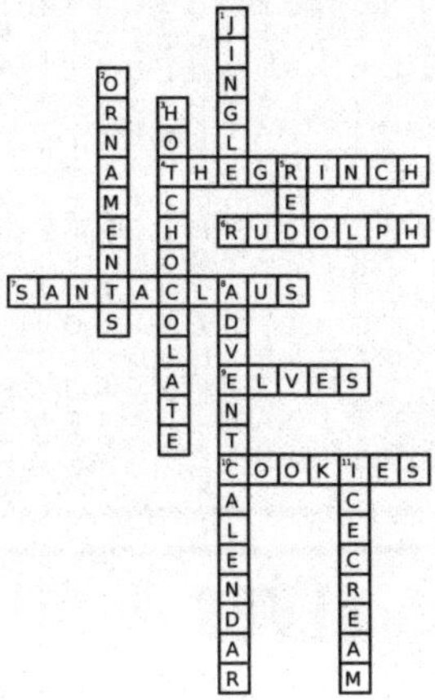

REINDEER RECOLLECTION

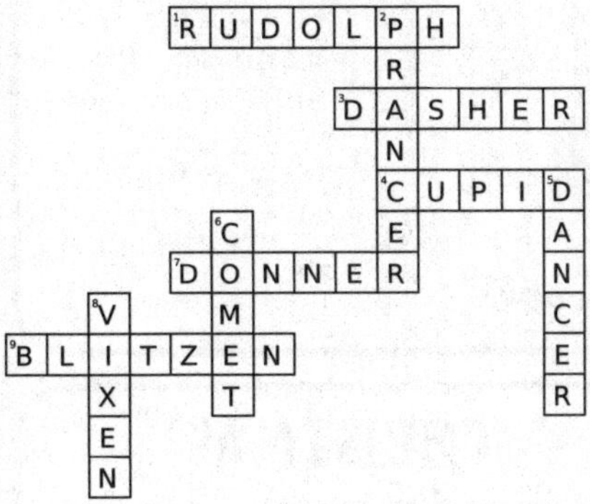

SUPER SANTA

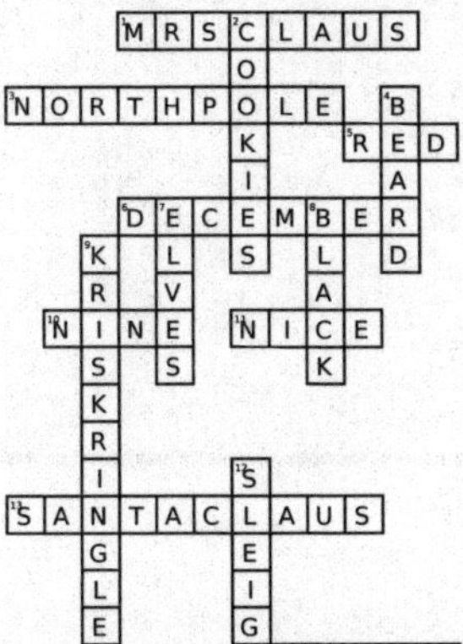

CHRISTMAS GIFTS

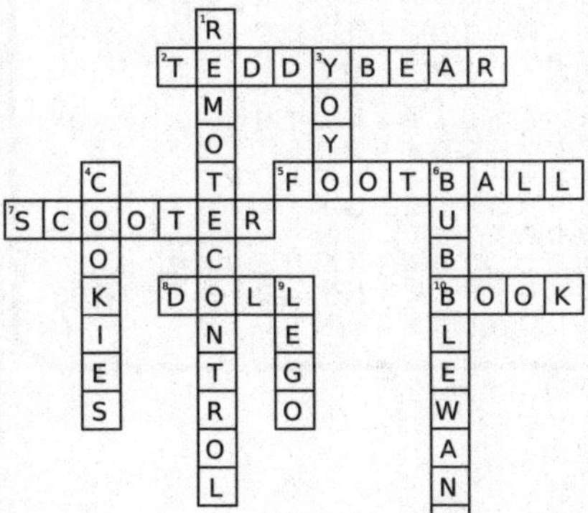

SUMMER CHRISTMAS

CHRISTMAS FOOD

CHRISTMAS

ELVES

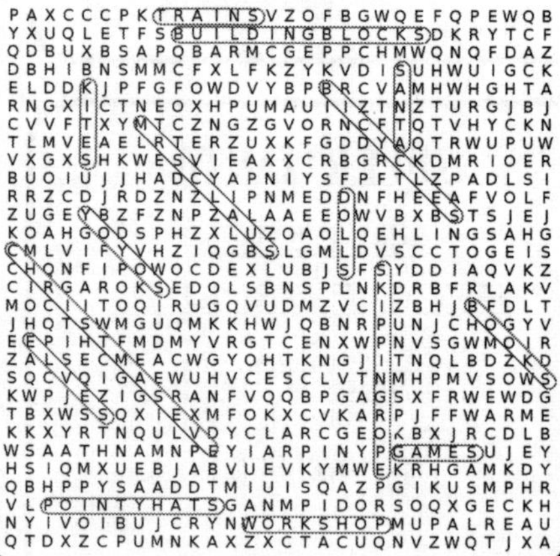

CHRISTMAS QUIZ ANSWERS: Q1: B) 25 December; Q2: Saint Nicholas, Kris Kringle, Father Christmas; Q3: The North Pole; Q4: The elves (supervised by Mrs Claus); Q5: Gingerbread; Q6: Twice; Q7: B) Christmas tree; Q8: Rudolph; Q9: Rudolph, Dasher, Dancer, Prancer, Vixen, Comet, Cupid, Donner, Blitzen; Q10: A) Stockings; Q11: Rudolph; Q12: Red.

PENGUIN BOOKS

UK | USA | Canada | Ireland | Australia
India | New Zealand | South Africa | China

Penguin Random House Australia is part of the Penguin Random House group of companies whose addresses can be found at global.penguinrandomhouse.com.

First published by Penguin Books, an imprint of Penguin Random House Australia Pty Ltd, in 2024

Cover and internal design and illustrations by Rebecca King © Penguin Random House Australia Pty Ltd

Internal icons: All background pattern icons and An A to Z of Christmas icons © Tiwat K/ Shutterstock.com; Tongue Twister, Santa Q&A and Rudolph Q&A speech bubbles © nubenamo/Shutterstock.com.

Printed and bound in Australia by Griffin Press, an accredited ISO AS/NZS 14001 Environmental Management Systems printer

NATIONAL LIBRARY OF AUSTRALIA

A catalogue record for this book is available from the National Library of Australia

FSC www.fsc.org MIX Paper | Supporting responsible forestry FSC® C018684

ISBN 978 1 76 134976 8 (Paperback)

Penguin Random House Australia uses papers that are natural and recyclable products, made from wood grown in sustainable forests. The logging and manufacture processes are expected to conform to the environmental regulations of the country of origin.

penguin.com.au

We at Penguin Random House Australia acknowledge that Aboriginal and Torres Strait Islander peoples are the Traditional Custodians and the first storytellers of the lands on which we live and work. We honour Aboriginal and Torres Strait Islander peoples' continuous connection to Country, waters, skies and communities. We celebrate Aboriginal and Torres Strait Islander stories, traditions and living cultures; and we pay our respects to Elders past and present.